JOHN WARD
COLORADO
MAGNIFICENT WILDERNESS

PHOTOGRAPHS
BY
JOHN WARD

FOREWORD
BY
JOHN FIELDER

Of the first edition of
Colorado, Magnificent Wilderness
seven hundred copies have been
made with hand-selected sheets,
specially bound, slipcased, numbered
and signed by John Ward.

John Ward 507

WESTCLIFFE PUBLISHERS, INC.
ENGLEWOOD, COLORADO

First frontispiece: South Rock Creek, Gore Range – Eagles Nest Wilderness.

Second frontispiece: Ghost town rainbow over Animas Forks.

Third frontispiece: Independence Monument, Colorado National Monument.

Below: Pink Bergamot decorates summer meadows near Boulder.

International Standard Book No.:
ISBN 0-942394-07-0

Library of Congress Catalog Card Number:
83-051395

Copyright: John Ward, 1984

Designer: Jerry Simpson

Printer: Dai Nippon Printing Co. Ltd.,
Tokyo, Japan

Publisher: Westcliffe Publishers, Inc.,
3900 South Windermere Street,
Englewood, Colorado 80110

As in all forms of artistic expression, photography provides us a view of ourselves, our environment, and the relationship between the two. Though the art form can be abstract, it is known best for its ability to portray realism, to present a view of the world as we conventionally understand it. Yet the mechanics of the camera and its films do allow for abstract expression. Photography in black and white best allows this expression by providing the artist a means with which to create images in his mind's eye. A blue scarf, a yellow melon, and a green tree take on shades of gray that allow the viewer to focus more clearly upon form, shape, and texture. Color for the sake of color in the image is not relevant to the purpose of the image.

Through our eyes our brains perceive color, for we live in a chromatic environment. Color to many of us is a constant joy, a source of daily pleasure, and often the reason why we use the words *beautiful* and *brilliant* in our language. In color photography, texture and shape often are secondary to the thrust of the image; the colors themselves and the way in which they relate to one another determine the success of the image on film. Yet unless one alters the film's perception of color, sometimes done using filters, the color artist can only render an exact image of what he sees. Except for the imagination of what one would like to see, there is not prior creation in the eye of one's mind.

So what does the color photographic artist do beyond preserving the reality of the moment on a piece of film? Initially there is perception. The visual sense is acute and constantly vigilant. The eyes isolate shape and form and texture within the chaos of the environment. One sees colors juxtaposed in ways and in combinations that please the senses. The task is simply to recognize when color, shape, and texture all complement one another with felicity and unprecedented singularity. The artist is no less

than perspicacious.

A revolution is occurring within the field of landscape photography. Color imagery is no longer just the possession of slickly laminated postcards depicting vistas neatly framed by colorful tree branches. Those at the forefront of the profession are showing the world a new way of perceiving and enjoying the visual aspects of the earth's landscape. We all appreciate the vastness of our planet and we tend to remark at those images depicting large portions of sky and land, or endless forests, or rivers meandering to infinity, or beaches lit by a setting sun. But what is there to see if we look inward, if we limit our landscape to just what we would see looking out of a window from the middle of the room into the forest? We would see just the trunks of trees, maybe too low to see green leaves, and certainly too narrow of a view to see sky or land. We would be viewing what the great landscape photographer, Eliot Porter, calls the "intimate landscape", a landscape not impressive for its use of infinity, but for the integrity it lends to one magnificent part of nature. These "intimate landscapes" are ubiquitous and our ability to perceive them is strictly a function of the perceptiveness of our eyes.

John Ward perceives both the spectacle of the broad landscape and nature's understated manifestations of color and form; yet he clearly prefers to photograph the latter. As you move through his journey through the seasons, you will begin to appreciate the more subtle aspects of the landscape, and when you reach the end of his journey you will better understand all that can be enjoyed within our wilderness environment. Your life will be touched by the vision of this photographer, not only from the experience of seeing his work, but because he has helped you to better perceive your own environment.

JOHN FIELDER

Colorado! Spanish for red after the great river that begins high in the Never Summer Range on the west side of Rocky Mountain National Park. Perhaps Spanish ears hear *Colorado* as just another ordinary word and maybe children growing up in metro Denver think nothing about it. But for me, even in its Anglicized pronunciation, Colorado has always been special. A special sound. A special place.

This is possibly the heritage of being non-native to the state, of hearing about it before ever seeing any of it. Happily, my family moved to Denver when I was ten and settled into a new house on the edge of the city. On a typical day one could look in a great arc from Long's Peak to the north, southward to Pike's Peak. This was in the fifties before the Valley Highway and before another million people came to dull the air with tailpipes and stovepipes. I took pictures then, usually of the summit and from the summit, but it never occurred to me that a photograph could be more than a trip record. That would come later along with greater appreciation of the landscape from trailhead to timberline.

This book is a product of that appreciation, an appreciation that has matured from an early passion for high places to a growing awareness of the aesthetic possibilities in undisturbed lands everywhere. These possibilities include beauty and solitude. And sometimes bleakness. The land may lie along a road or on the edge of a city. As such the land is not wild for bears or even humans but it does nicely for chipmunks, butterflies and other small creatures.

The magnificent wilderness of this book is thus larger than the legally circumscribed tracts now called Wilderness Areas. This is not to denigrate Wilderness Areas in any way; these lie at the emotional and aesthetic core of all that is in the book. Not too long ago, only a few generations really, all of Colorado was wild and even within the time of my own residency much of the

mountainous part was little used and relatively wild. The Wilderness Areas thus represent a singular step by one generation to preserve for future generations what was taken for granted less than a quarter of a century ago. But the idea of wild land and its tonic properties for urbanized mankind goes beyond Congressional edict. Future generations will be shortchanged if we do not strive to manage all our land areas with respect for the special sensibilities of wilderness, if not for the bears, then at least for the butterflies.

The photographs in this book have been made over a period of a dozen years yet they consititute a very particular view of Colorado wilderness. Principally it is an intermediate view, the quiet special moments of wilderness at five to fifty feet, large enough to see without crawling around on the ground looking under rocks and small enough to walk past without ever noticing.

Intrepid caption readers will note some imbalances in what is presented. For example, a single image comes from the Great Plains while the Rocky Mountain National Park, Weminuche and Maroon Bells-Snowmass areas figure prominently. On the other hand, three "Halfmoon" pictures come from three distinct areas with two different spellings no less. A somewhat curious phenomenon is what I call the clumping of photographs. A book doesn't just happen. Whether rightly or wrongly, every page is carefully thought out. In the present case images were selected on the basis of how they looked together. Sometimes variations on a theme and at other times formal or chromatic considerations were paramount. Nonetheless, it is remarkable in the final sequence how often photographs from the same area, even though taken years apart, appeared on successive or nearby pages. I eschew all metaphysical considerations yet remain at a loss for more deterministic explanations.

This thought, however, reminds me of Ansel Adams' famous dictum that sometimes he felt he arrived at places just when God wanted a photograph. In my own work I have often decried the lack of divine intervention as light failed or wind came up just as I was cocking the shutter. More insidiously, many a cloud has crept into a corner between my last look at an image on the ground glass and the taking of the picture precious seconds later. The reader unacquainted with matters photographic must understand that at its very fastest, which usually entails a degree of recklessness, view camera photography is painfully slow compared to the simple pleasures of 35mm or Instamatic photography. No matter. At times I have been very fortunate and for these special moments remain forever thankful.

On one such occasion a rainbow appeared as I was bumping my way down Engineer Pass towards Animas Forks in the company of my faithful field assistant, also known as my wife, Susan. Rainbows are special for all romantic photographers and not just any old foreground would do. Keeping in mind that in four-wheel driving I much prefer to creep than leap, and that my 8"x10" camera was nestled in a foam pad but otherwise loose in the back of our pickup, I proceeded as rapidly as I dared, searching desperately for a suitable composition. Normally, old foundations do not position themselves conveniently under rainbows but as we pulled into Animas Forks with the light beginning to fail I remembered walking around a particular foundation looking in vain for an interesting image the previous year. Now I knew exactly what to do. I had about sixty seconds, maybe ninety, in which to yank down the tailgate, grab the 4"x5" camera, stumble down a steep embankment, position the tripod on irregular ground, set up the camera and make the exposure. Without question I could not have succeeded without Susan's skillful help in grabbing the focusing cloth, the light meter and, most important of all, the right film holder. The cognoscenti will note in the above narrative that I metered the light.

Haphazard as it was, this was necessary because there was no moon.

Another occasion worth noting lacked the high drama of the preceding episode but is even more remarkable for the finely etched memories of a glorious morning as fog repeatedly rolled in and out of Colorado National Monument. We were on the way home from a short trip to Canyonlands and as we proceeded at dusk along Utah 128, a good dirt road in those days, the plan was to drive all night back to Boulder. On the high desert near Cisco we ran into pea-soup fog which was quite a novelty at first but quickly proved tiresome as we groped our way east. Still in fog at Fruita, we changed plans and headed for the campground at Colorado National Monument which took us up out of the fog into a clear black night. The next morning I peeked out of the tent, saw the valley full of clouds and got up as quickly as one can manage on a cold morning in a very small tent with frozen boots and frosty glasses. It is an occupational hazard in photography that at times one must work with such intensity and speed that in the end, even though many fine images have been made, there is no coherent memory of the event. That morning began in such a fashion but after the first couple of images, the wonder of it all asserted itself and by midmorning I had decided the experience was so enchanting that it didn't make any difference how the film came out. I am pleased, of course, that some of the film came out rather well but mostly I treasure the memory of standing on the rim beside my camera watching the fog drift in.

There are special moments in Colorado's wilderness for everyone willing to pause and look for them, whether in a field of flowers, a pattern of leaves on a boulder or some magnificent panorama. This book is for all who love the land but I dedicate it to Susan who taught me appreciation for the land beside the trail and who likes watching the fog drift in.

JOHN WARD

Out of browns and white, Spring begins with a bit of blue water in long frozen lakes and streams, and continues as a delicate greening slowly climbs its way from plains and foothills to high mountain peak, followed by the rich greens and the bright wildflower colors of a new season.

❦

Molas Lake reflects the icy mantle of the Grenadier Range (previous page) while in Rocky Mountain National Park the Fall River glides around golden rocks below Mt. Chapin.

*In Rocky Mountain National Park
the Big Thompson River gradually
melts as a dead Spruce brightens the
muted colors of early Spring along
the Fern Lake Trail.*

Claret Cup Cactus blooms beside a fallen Pinyon Pine in Monument Canyon at Colorado National Monument. Across the state, catkins herald the arrival of Spring in the northern Front Range.

Small transient icebergs mimic boulders along the shore of The Loch as ice floes chill Sky Pond below Powell Peak, both in Rocky Mountain National Park.

In a wet Spring, water cascades down the walls of Clear Creek Canyon west of Golden. To the north, beavers have made new ponds near the beginning of the Glacier Gorge Trail in Rocky Mountain National Park.

Near Boulder, Apples blossom and Lilacs bloom in Gregory Canyon just before One-sided Penstemon (overleaf) adds color to fields below the rocky Flatirons.

*Sunlight and time color an
old mining ruin near Animas Forks.
Stonecrop brightens rocky ledges
throughout the mountains.*

A misty waterfall is hidden near Weller Lake in the White River National Forest. In Rocky Mountain National Park a Lodgepole Pine forest stands quietly in Horseshoe Park and (overleaf) the Big Thompson River meanders through Moraine Park.

*On a rainy afternoon the state
flower, Colorado Blue Columbine,
grows beside a stand of Aspen
scarred by Elk seeking winter forage,
both in Rocky Mountain
National Park.*

*To the highest crags, Summer may
journey only once every few years
but when alpine flowers dot the
marshy tundra and marmots laze in
the morning sun before a chill
afternoon thundershower, and alpine
glow lights the distant peaks
above a hot dry plain,
Summer has come to Colorado.*

❦

*Marshmarigolds cover an alpine
meadow below Snowmass Mountain
in the Maroon Bells – Snowmass
Wilderness. Overleaf: A heavy
winter snowpack lingers on the pass
to Hasley Basin as seen from
Frigid Air Pass.*

*In the Maroon Bells – Snowmass
Wilderness an intricate stump decays
along Snowmass Creek
while Pyramid Peak looms beyond
Minnehaha Gulch. Overleaf:
To the south in the Weminuche
Wilderness a full moon sets over
Eldorado Lake.*

Salmon Lake nestles below the Gore Range in the Gore Range – Eagles Nest Wilderness. Threatening clouds arch over a tundra pool on the flanks of Mt. Audubon in the Indian Peaks Wilderness.

Snowmelt and summer showers bring colorful wildflowers to the Gunnison National Forest and send Notch Mountain Creek rushing down from Half Moon Pass in the Holy Cross Wilderness.

*Glacial boulders preface Blue Lake
and Mt. Toll in the Indian Peaks
Wilderness. Further west, the
Maroon Bells rise above a soggy
meadow below Willow Pass.
Overleaf: Gentle twilight engulfs The
Guardian and Mt. Silex in the
Weminuche Wilderness.*

*Lush tundra carpets the terrain
north of Kite Lake as North Clear
Creek Falls tumbles over the edge of
an old lava flow, both in the Rio
Grande National Forest.*

Silvery patterns in an old stump along Halfmoon Creek in the San Isabel National Forest echo a maze of giant spires produced by erosion of volcanic tuft in Wheeler Geologic Area.

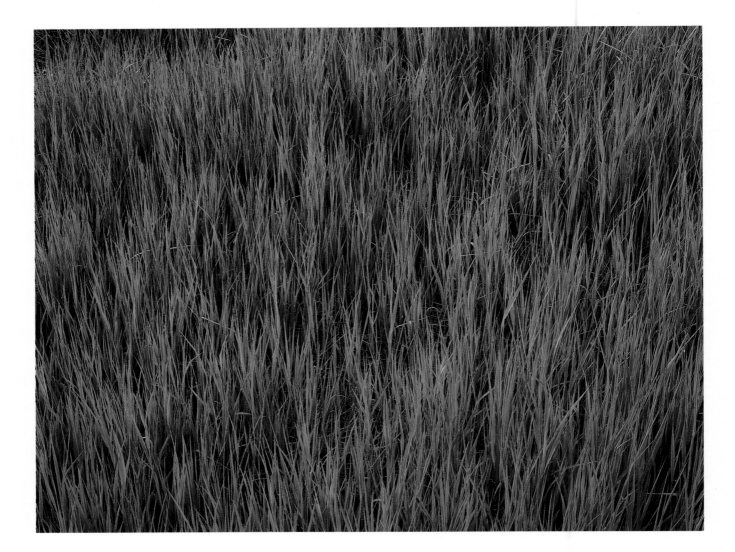

*Moods of Summer: verdant grasses
grow below Kite Lake in the
Rio Grande National Forest as swirls
of sand mark a graceful crest in
Great Sand Dunes National
Monument and (overleaf) a rare fog
envelops the forest on Flagstaff
Mountain near Boulder.*

*Trunks, roots and boulders hobnob
below Ouzel Falls in Rocky
Mountain National Park. In the
Weminuche Wilderness, Needle
Creek flows past mossy boulders in
a soft green forest and
(overleaf) the setting sun inflames
clouds above the Continental Divide
near Hunchback Mountain.*

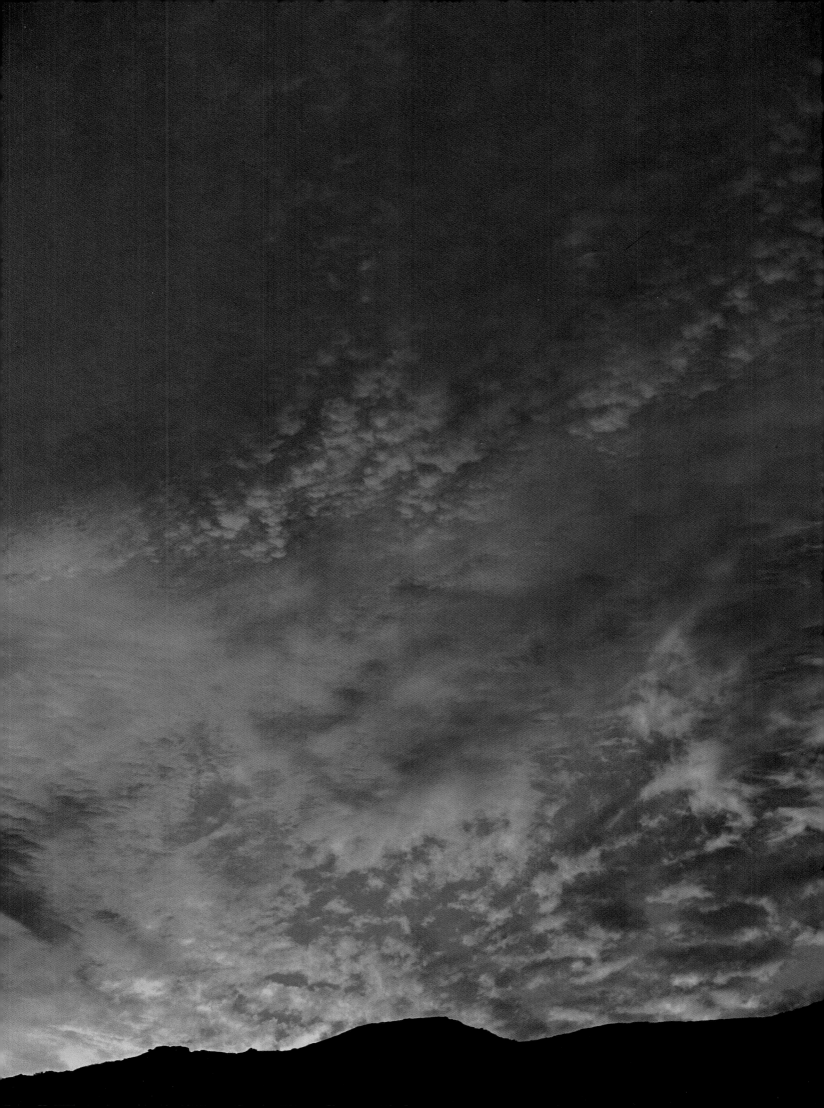

*Lichens and leaves share a
boulder beside the Lawn Lake Trail
in Rocky Mountain National Park.
The brighter colors of Paintbrush and
Cinquefoil are found on Halfmoon
Pass in the La Garita Wilderness.*

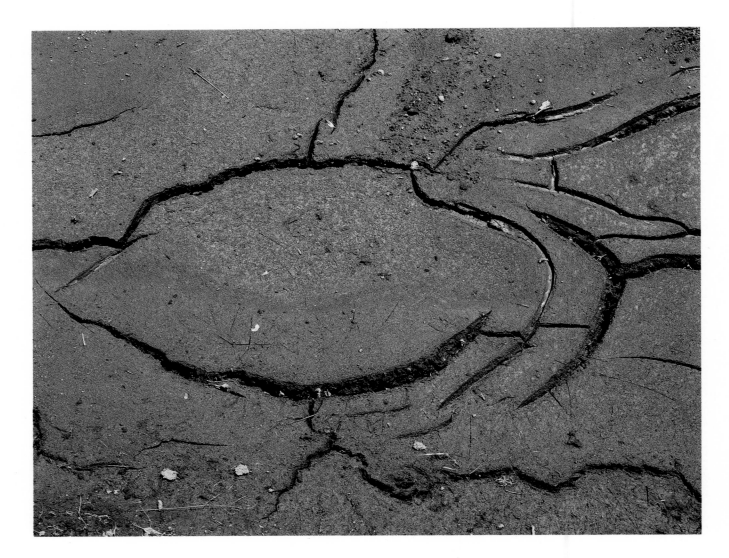

Quizzical patterns appear in mudcracks at the summit of Tincup Pass and in the wood of Bristlecone Pines near Blue Park in the Rio Grande National Forest.

*Contrasts in green: Sumac leaves
after a summer rain along
the Bluebell Trail near Boulder and
Englemann Spruce on the Gore
Range Trail in Arapaho National
Forest.*

*In Routt National Forest, Paintbrush
and Lupine add color to a meadow
near Dumont Lake. Maryland Creek
is a small trickle where it crosses the
Gore Range Trail in Arapaho
National Forest.*

Fallen Aspen litter the meadow along Cub Lake Trail and burned Lodgepole Pines above Ouzel Falls begin the cycle of renewal wrought by wildfire, both in Rocky Mountain National Park. Overleaf: Beyond Engineer Mountain lies the Uncompahgre Wilderness.

Ephemeral patterns grace a window
screen at Mineral Point Mill in the
Uncompahgre National Forest. A few
miles away the old mansion still
stands at Animas Forks.

A chill wind blows from summits down rugged canyons to foothills and plain; an exposed ridge bursts into gold and then a tree here and another there and soon a whole mountainside glows brightly in the noonday sun. The word goes out: the Aspen are turning and Autumn is here.

❧

Aspen highlight the Rio Grande Gorge above Ute Creek in the Rio Grande National Forest.

Aspen patterns appear against an azure sky west of Lake City and against the shadowed flanks of Pyramid Peak in the Maroon Bells – Snowmass Wilderness. Overleaf: An Aspen stand is suffused with the soft glow of reflected gold.

Floating leaves enrich a quiet pool in Rocky Mountain National Park as Sumac brightens the Bluebell Trail west of Boulder.

*Red Aspen contrast with green and
gold near Kebler Pass in
Gunnison National Forest while Oak
and Cottonwoods turn in the lower
valleys near Paonia.*

*Aspen crown a small ridge
near Crater Lake in Maroon Bells –
Snowmass Wilderness. On the east
slope in Rocky Mountain National
Park the Big Thompson River drifts
among golden grasses under blue
skies. Overleaf: A palette of color on
the Grand Mesa.*

Sun shines on Kinikinick and Juniper near Lake Helene in Rocky Mountain National Park. In the Rio Grande National Forest the ground is drenched after a sudden shower.

The colors of Autumn: yellows in an old Aspen stand in Rocky Mountain National Park, reds in a younger stand near Lost Lake in the Gunnison National Forest and (overleaf) a rich variety on a hillside above Paonia Reservoir.

*Red Sumac and golden Ash occur
within a few yards of one another in
Gregory Canyon west of Boulder.*

*Aspen leaves scatter across an
ancient boulder. Fallen leaves and
fallen metal surround an old cabin at
the Argo Mill in Idaho Springs.*

Finally the last leaf falls, the temperature drops and Winter comes, sometimes with a howl and sometimes quietly in the night, as the flakes drift down faster and faster and pile higher and higher. And in the light of a cold clear day, forest, meadow and mountain all rest peacefully under the snow.

❦

A Ponderosa Pine stands tall in Winter's first snow.

*Twigs catch fresh snow in a partially
frozen pool while at higher elevations
the winds of winter ripple ice on a
pond. Overleaf: First light on new
snow in the lower foothills near
Boulder.*

Icy gales sweep across the
Continental Divide above Cub Lake
in Rocky Mountain National Park.
Lower foothill streams may flow
much of the Winter in some years.

On a clear day open water reflects the plains landscape in Morgan County. After the storm, Boulder's Third Flatiron basks in morning sunlight.

*The quiet days of Winter stretch
across Monument Canyon in
Colorado National Monument as fog
blankets the Grand Valley beyond.*

*The green needles of Ponderosa Pines
dusted lightly with snow give promise
of yet another Spring.*